It's CHRISTMAS!

ALL ABOUT
CHRISTMAS CAROLS

KRISTEN RAJCZAK NELSON

PowerKiDS press™

NEW YORK

Published in 2020 by The Rosen Publishing Group, Inc.
29 East 21st Street, New York, NY 10010

First Edition

Editor: Kristen Rajczak Nelson
Book Design: Reann Nye

Photo Credits: Cover © www.istockphoto.com/Juanmonino; p. 5 © www.istockphoto.com/izusek; p. 7 PHAS/Universal Images Group/Getty Images; p. 9 Universal History Archive/Universal Images Group/Getty Images; p. 11 Zvonimir Atletic/Shutterstock.com; p. 13 Culture Club/Hulton Archive/Getty Images; p. 15 Print Collector/Hulton Archive/Getty Images; p. 17 © www.istockphoto.com/gameover2012; p. 19 New Africa/Shutterstock.com; p. 21 © www.istockphoto.com/whitemay; p. 22 Dream_Stock/Shutterstock.com.

Cataloging-in-Publication Data
Names: Rajczak Nelson, Kristen.
Title: All about Christmas carols / Kristen Rajczak Nelson.
Description: New York : PowerKids Press, 2020. | Series: It's Christmas! | Includes glossary and index.
Identifiers: ISBN 9781725300682 (pbk.) | ISBN 9781725300705 (library bound) | ISBN 9781725300699 (6pack)
Subjects: LCSH: Christmas music–History and criticism–Juvenile literature. | Carols–History and criticism–Juvenile literature. | Carols-Juvenile literature.
Classification: LCC ML2880.R35 2020 | DDC 782.28'1723–dc23

CPSIA Compliance Information: Batch #CSPK19. For Further Information contact Rosen Publishing, New York, New York at 1-800-237-9932.

CONTENTS

HARK! CAROLS TO SING 4

O COME ALL YE FAITHFUL.............. 8

HERE WE COME A WASSAILING......... 12

SILENT NIGHTS 14

DECK THE HALLS! 16

JOY TO THE WORLD.................. 22

GLOSSARY 23

INDEX 24

WEBSITES 24

HARK! CAROLS TO SING

Nothing puts everyone in the Christmas spirit more than Christmas music! Every December, radio stations and stores play hours of Christmas songs, from "Jingle Bells" to "Silent Night." But Christmas carols haven't always been so important to Christmas. In fact, the carols we sing today have been popular for less than 200 years!

The word "carol" is much older than Christmas carols. Hundreds of years ago, it meant a song that was used for special dances done in a ring or circle. Later, it came to mean a song that had two main parts, the refrain and **verse**. A refrain is words and music that are repeated.

O COME ALL YE FAITHFUL

Songs have long been part of winter **celebrations**. Groups in northern Europe marked the **winter solstice** with dancing, singing, food, and drink. When Christians spread to these areas, they combined these winter holidays with Christian ideas. The songs and celebrations weren't a part of Christmas right away, though.

For a long time, Christmas songs were written in Latin and only sung in churches. In the 13th century, a man called Francis of Assisi began using **religious** music in plays about the Christian Christmas story. The songs were to be sung in whatever language the common people spoke. They became **popular**!

11

HERE WE COME A WASSAILING

Singing songs to celebrate Christmas spread across Europe. This was combined with the **tradition** of wassailing. When wassailing, people would go from house to house looking for warmth and food or wishing good cheer to neighbors. Travelers began to sing as they went door to door. Today we call this caroling!

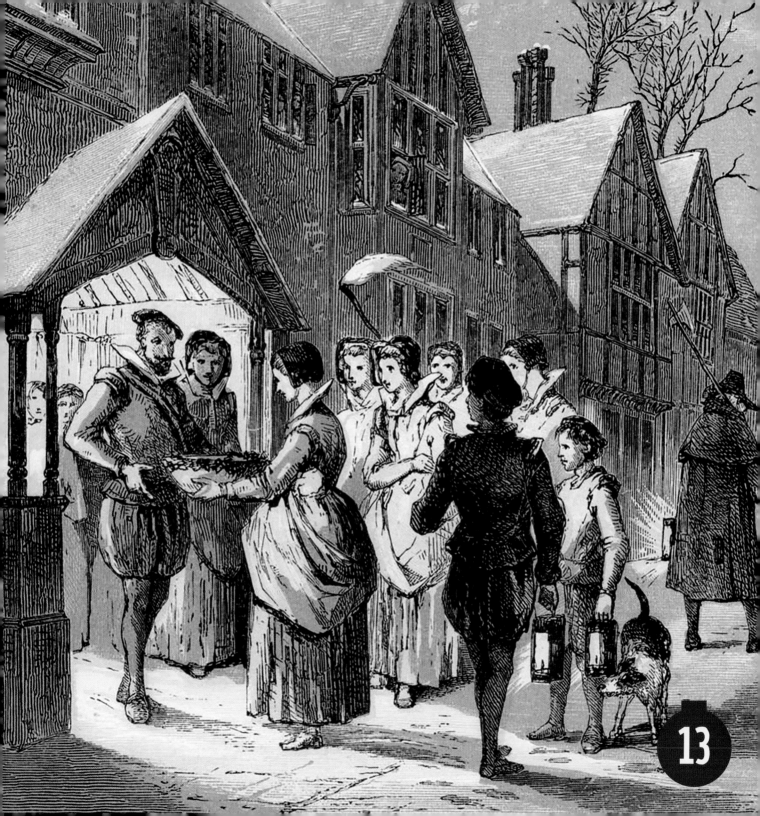

SILENT NIGHTS

Christmas carols became important religious music in the **Middle Ages**. However, during the 1600s, some groups in England stopped allowing celebrations of Christmas like wassailing. Traditions were kept up in some villages, but they lost public popularity. Then, in 1840, Queen Victoria of England married Prince Albert, who was German.

DECK THE HALLS!

Germany had many traditions for its winter holiday, called Yule or Yuletide, including songs and **decorated** trees. Prince Albert shared these with the queen, mixing them with the English Christmas holiday. The people of England **adopted** these traditions and our modern Christmas celebration was born.

16

As Christmas celebrations became widespread, people wrote more carols. Many of the most well-known carols sung today—such as "Silent Night," "Joy to the World," and "Jolly Old St. Nicholas"—were written during the mid- to late 1800s. Older religious carols were written out in English around this time, too.

Christmas carols were now an important part of Christmastime. Caroling again gained popularity. By the early 1900s, books of caroling music started coming out, making these songs even more available to the public. One of these collections, called the *Oxford Book of Carols*, had 201 carols in it!

21

JOY TO THE WORLD

Today, it's more common to see carolers at the mall than going door to door. But, Christmas carols are still a big part of church services and holiday celebrations in many schools and homes. Whether around the tree or in your neighborhood, carols are always a fun part of the Christmas season!

GLOSSARY

adopt: To take on as one's own.

celebration: A party or special event held to mark a holiday.

decorate: To make something look nice by adding something to it.

Middle Ages: A time in Europe from about AD 500 to 1500.

popular: The state of being liked by many people.

religious: Having to do with religion, or a belief in a god or gods.

tradition: A way of thinking or doing something within a group of people.

verse: Part of a poem or song.

winter solstice: The shortest day of the year.

INDEX

A
Albert, Prince, 14, 16

C
Christians, 8, 10

D
dance, 6, 8

E
England, 14, 16
English (language), 18
Europe, 8, 12

F
Francis of Assisi, 10

G
Germany, 16

J
"Jingle Bells," 4
"Jolly Old St. Nicholas," 18
"Joy to the World," 18

L
Latin, 10

M
Middle Ages, 14

O
Oxford Book of Carols, 20

P
plays, 10

S
"Silent Night," 4, 18

V
Victoria, Queen, 14, 16

W
wassailing, 12, 14
winter solstice, 8

Y
Yuletide (Yule), 16

WEBSITES

Due to the changing nature of Internet links, PowerKids Press has developed an online list of websites related to the subject of this book. This site is updated regularly. Please use this link to access the list: www.powerkidslinks.com/IC/carols